Original title:
Succulents and Sunshine

Copyright © 2025 Creative Arts Management OÜ
All rights reserved.

Author: Helena Marchant
ISBN HARDBACK: 978-1-80581-885-4
ISBN PAPERBACK: 978-1-80581-412-2
ISBN EBOOK: 978-1-80581-885-4

Arid Beauty in Radiant Days

In pots of green, they sit so proud,
With leaves like smiles, they cheer out loud.
Water once, then leave them be,
Cacti dance, wild and free.

They soak up rays, a little too much,
Waving their arms, they love the touch.
While folks complain of summer's heat,
These prickly pals just can't be beat.

No fear of rain, they'll never drown,
In desert garb, they wear the crown.
Talk of a drought? They just laugh it off,
They're tough little creatures, never scoff.

So here's to bright days, plants in a row,
They thrive on neglect, put on quite a show.
With style and grace, they sway in the sun,
In their dry little world, they always have fun.

Nature's Sunny Embrace

In pots, they wiggle, dance, and sway,
With smiles that brighten up the day.
They soak the rays, oh what a sight,
Who knew my plants could feel so bright?

A little water is all they seek,
Yet never speak, they play hide and peek.
With spiky hats and colors bold,
My silent crew, they're pure gold!

Potted Joy in Sunlit Corners

Green little creatures, in their lair,
Chasing dust motes through the air.
They wink at me with leafy charms,
In sunlit corners, raising alarms!

A cactus grins, a succulent sings,
Who knew plants could have such things?
They gossip 'bout the sun's bright gleam,
While I just sip and start to dream.

Warm Hues of Living Green

With shades of jade and subtle blush,
In my garden, there's never a rush.
They giggle softly in the heat,
And dance to rhythms, oh so sweet!

Potting soil sprinkled with glee,
They prance around, as sprightly as can be.
In warm hues, they find their groove,
Making lawn chairs feel like a move!

The Garden's Luminous Embrace

At twilight's call, they glow so bright,
Reflecting mischief in the night.
A wall of green, with whispers low,
They plot the next delightful show!

With cheeks of coral and spears of jade,
They steal the limelight, unafraid.
As stars peep through, they share a wink,
In nature's laugh, we all will sink!

Golden Embrace

In the window's glow, they sit with flair,
Lazing about without a single care.
With a twisty leaf, they strike a pose,
Sunshine's warmth, their secret knows.

They giggle as the day drifts by,
Whispers of green, a sly little sigh.
In pots so small, they hold such might,
Tiny warriors basking in the light.

Drifting in Radiance

Sipping on rays, they tilt and sway,
Chasing shadows, come what may.
With plump little cheeks, they seem to grin,
Knowing all the fun that's about to begin.

Bending and bowing, they tell quite a tale,
Of sun-soaked dreams and a gentle gale.
In this garden world, laughter fills the space,
Joyfully thriving in their sunny embrace.

Flora and Rays

Little green folks with a favorite game,
Competing for sunlight, but who's to blame?
They stretch their limbs in a silly ballet,
As if to say, 'We're brightening your day!'

Be careful, dear friend; don't knock them down,
They might just sprout legs and dance around.
With a wink from a leaf, they plot their spree,
In the warmth of the sun, they're wild and free.

Sunlit Prickles

With a fuzzy crown and a prickly grin,
These spiky guys know how to win.
They bask in glory, no need for disguise,
Rays set them laughing with twinkly eyes.

"Oh, look at us, we're quite the sight!"
Sharing joy in the soft daylight.
With tiny flowers that nod in cheer,
Each day is a party; come join us here!

Prickles and Petals in Day's Embrace

In a garden where oddities grow,
A cactus in dance steals the show.
With a wig made of moss and a grin,
It pricks at the sun, but still wants to win.

Petals in hues that tickle your nose,
A daisy in stripes, pretending it flows.
Laughing at bees that forget their own route,
While sipping on nectar like a sprightly scout.

Bright Echoes of Verdant Life

In pots of mischief, they all reside,
A plant with a dance and a quirky slide.
It sways to the chimes of a passing breeze,
Winking at sunbeams with effortless ease.

One leaf naps sprawled on a sunny chair,
While others have formed quite the playful dare.
Bidding the ants to do the conga line,
As light trickles down, where they intertwine.

Vistas of Vibrancy

Oh, look at that bloom, what a sight to behold,
Wearing a tutu, it's brave and it's bold.
With colors that pop like confetti at play,
In the court of green critters, they dance all day.

Chasing the clouds with a head held up high,
While giggling at birds that just swoosh by.
The joy of each leaf, a whimsical spree,
Whispering secrets, just you and me.

Light-Kissed Leaves

In the arms of the sun, they bask with delight,
With shades that could start a colorful fight.
Each time a breeze whispers a fleeting tune,
They sway with abandon, a leafy festoon.

One sprout wears glasses, calling it classy,
While another insists it's the world that's sassy.
Together they sing in a choir so bright,
Creating a ruckus from morning till night.

Verdant Resilience Beneath the Sky

In pots of clay, they gather cheer,
With sassy smiles, they persevere.
A water drop? They say, 'Oh please!'
We thrive on laughs, not on your frees.

Spiky blooms and shades of green,
Who needs a shower? That's so mean!
We're cuddly plants, tough as nails,
In sunlit dreams, we weave our tales.

Petals of Light

Look at us, we soak the rays,
In silly hats, we dance and sway.
A cactus pricks, but don't you pout,
We're the party, without a doubt.

With shades of pink and hints of blue,
We sip on sunlight, feeling new.
Don't water us too much, my friend,
Or we'll throw a fit that won't just end.

Desert Dreams in Bloom

We're the rebels of the sand,
Dancing coyly, so unplanned.
Each bloom's a giggle in the air,
A prickly joke? We simply dare.

In heat we flourish, thrive and grin,
A daily race to look within.
We barter with the blazing sun,
And wink at clouds that want to run.

Lush Life Under the Sun

Underneath that blazing glow,
We wear our charm, and steal the show.
With every leaf, a punchline shared,
No garden gnome left unimpaired.

In pots we plot our jolly schemes,
With roots in soil, we chase our dreams.
Forget the rules, we're here to play,
In our vibrant world, it's always May.

Resilient Beauty

In a pot, a plant does sway,
It giggles at the light of day.
With leaves so plump and bright, they tease,
It drinks from rain and feels the breeze.

When friends stop by they often gawk,
At green delights that seem to talk.
"Water me? Oh please, not too!"
They laugh, it's true, they just want you.

With roots so firm and humor stout,
This little green thing knows no doubt.
It cheers me up with every glance,
In its own way, it loves to dance.

A resilient spirit, bold and spry,
This jolly flora reaches high.
If only humans caught the hint,
Life should be fun, not just a sprint.

Cactus Dreams

In a dream, a cactus wore a hat,
Doing cha-cha on the welcome mat.
With little spikes that jiggle and jive,
It threw a party that felt alive.

A disco ball hung from its thorn,
Playing tunes from dusk till dawn.
The desert critters danced with cheer,
While the sunlit charm drew them near.

"Come on, folks! You can't resist!"
It yelled, waving spiky fists.
From every corner, they joined the splay,
In a botanical balletic ballet!

So when you roam where cacti grow,
Watch for a soirée that's sure to glow.
With prickly pals and mirth aflight,
They'll dance with you till the morning light.

Warmth Among the Spikes

Amidst the rough, the soft does thrive,
A cheerful plant that's so alive.
With sunny vibes and quirky looks,
It breaks the rules in all the books.

"Don't poke me, friend, I'm more than thorns!"
It giggles in the light of morns.
With laughter in its leafy tongue,
Having fun while it's still young.

In gardens where the sunshine beams,
A quirky world of greenish dreams.
With every ray, a smile it shares,
Among the spikes, no room for cares.

So take a moment, raise your glass,
To plants that breathe and seem to laugh.
With warmth wrapped in a spiky guise,
They teach us well to improvise.

The Color of Calm

A pot of green, a sight so sweet,
With little hues at every heat.
It nods its head, a mellow muse,
In each bright shade, a hint to choose.

Chillin' in the window sun,
This funky plant is all about fun.
"Feeling stressed? Just take a peek!"
It beckons with a tongue-in-cheek.

Its leaves are shades of light and bold,
Stories of laughter yet untold.
A dash of humor, calm to seek,
Between the greens, the playful speak.

So sit awhile, let worries slide,
With colors bright, come take a ride.
In every leaf, a story's woven,
A canvas bright where hearts are golden.

Desert Nurture

In the corner, you stand tall,
A little green, not much at all.
Your friends are tall, they laugh and play,
But I'm the one who saves the day.

I water once, but you hold tight,
In the sun, you steal the light.
Your little spikes, they poke and tease,
You're the pet that aims to please.

Sometimes I forget your shade,
But you don't care, you're not afraid.
A drought? Oh please, it's just a jest,
I'm thriving here, I'm truly blessed.

So here's to you, my leafy mate,
Our bond is weird, but it's first-rate.
You sip the sun like it's some brew,
And I just laugh, oh how you grew!

Radiance in Green

In a pot with soil so dry,
You stretch your arms up to the sky.
A drip of water? Not too much!
You love it mild, with just a touch.

Your pals around, so bright and bold,
Cacti that wear spikes like they're gold.
Yet here you are, in shades of jade,
Giving sass, while I just shade.

We dance in light, a silly sight,
You wink at me, and it feels right.
You wave your leaves, a goofy grin,
Oh, don't you start, let fun begin!

With every bloom, you show your flair,
In a world so bright beyond compare.
Let's toast to joy, and let it be,
With sunshine smiles and laughter free!

Lush Resilience

You're a wonder, in vibrant green,
Sipping sunbeams, a joyful scene.
What's that? A wilt? You'll be just fine,
For laughter flows in every line.

My watering can is getting light,
But you just smile, oh what a sight.
Your roots dig deep, you stand so proud,
A green comedian, drawing a crowd.

Each leaf a joke, each bloom a laugh,
You're the star of this sunny path.
While others bend and sometimes break,
Your humor blooms, for goodness' sake!

So raise a glass to joy in pots,
Let's cherish those quirky green spots.
In every crack, in every glee,
You thrive, dear plant, forever free!

Blossoms in the Light

Tiny petals in the glare,
You wave to friends without a care.
Your jokes are sweet, your vibes are bright,
In a world so green, what a delight!

It's a wonder how you grow,
Watered with laughter, don't you know?
Your puns are sharp as any thorns,
Yet bring us joy, like cheerful morns.

With every ray, you steal the show,
Making me giggle; it's a glow.
You whisper secrets to the breeze,
And charmingly dance between the leaves.

So here's to blooms and cheeky jest,
To those who flourish, none can best.
In every petal, every twist,
You find the fun, and we can't resist!

Hues of Humble Growth

In pots so round, they sit with pride,
Tiny warriors, with no need to hide.
With a wink and a twist, they stand so tall,
A quirky bunch, they just have a ball.

Water me, please, they cheer with glee,
But not too much, oh, let me be!
Their thirsty cries, a humorous sight,
A perfect blend of wrong and right.

With colors bright, they like to play,
Dancing in circles at the start of day.
Laughter blooms where leaves will sway,
These cheerful plants just rule the way.

Each little spine, a tale to tell,
In this gentle garden, all is swell.
With sunlight and giggles, they grow just fine,
In this riot of green, they truly shine.

Nature's Palette Against the Sky

Under the beam of a golden gleam,
Dancing colors in a vibrant dream.
A splash of green, a blob of pink,
These little wonders make us think.

With petals bright, they wave so free,
"Don't forget us!" they shout with glee.
In a world of colors, who needs paint?
When nature's artists, giggle, and faint!

Amongst the blue, they strike a pose,
With funny antics, who knows how it goes?
Plucking rays from above, they shout,
"Watch us sparkle! Come check us out!"

In this fun-filled garden, joy takes hold,
Where sunlight sparkles, and laughter's gold.
They wear the hues of a merry crew,
And relish the warmth as they break through.

Prickly Companions in Warmth

Meet the pals with a pointy flair,
In their gentle spikes, they hold their share.
Laughing through warmth, they stand so stout,
Prickly buddies, what's this about?

In a sunny nook, they plot and scheme,
"Let's take a nap, but first, a dream!"
They poke out tongues at the clumsy flies,
"Buzz off, dear friend! We've got sunny skies!"

They whisper secrets in the soft light,
Joking that they're ready to take flight.
With a chuckle, they drink their share,
Happily basking without a care.

So sit back and watch their shenanigans grow,
In the warmth of laughter, they steal the show.
With points like armor, they face the day,
Prickly pals in sunshine's play.

Roots of Resilience in Brightness

Deep down below, their roots laugh tight,
Grounding themselves with all their might.
As sunshine beams and shadows dance,
They spin their tales of a resilient chance.

"Stretch out!" they sing, "Feel the warm glow!
We're not just plants, we're stars of the show!"
Breathing in light like a big ol' joke,
With nature's humor, they gently poke.

Wiggly roots in a playful race,
Burrowing deep to find their place.
No fear of drought, they giggle and cheer,
In the face of dryness, they persevere!

With each bright leaf, a tale unfolds,
A dance with patience, humor so bold.
In a world that spins with laughter's art,
These roots remind us where to start.

Gleams of Green in the Warmth

Little plants in pots so bright,
Waving leaves in laughter's light.
Drinking sun like it's a treat,
Grinning wide, they can't be beat.

Poking tongues of green so spry,
With a twist, they wink goodbye.
In this cozy, sunny nook,
They plot mischief, take a look!

Growing strong without a hitch,
Telling secrets, making a pitch.
With a poke and playful tease,
They dance and sway in the warm breeze.

Who needs a gardener's care?
These little sprites, they're quite rare.
With their roots all snug and tight,
They giggle through the golden light.

Landscape of Light and Life

Behold a world of green delight,
Where every leaf is out of sight.
Bouncing round in pots so full,
They prank the shirt on gardener's pull.

With each ray, they stretch with glee,
Daring bees to come and see.
Whispers tease about their charms,
Making mischief, raising alarms.

Cacti wear their prickly hats,
Inviting giggles from the cats.
Tiny blooms, the jokers' play,
Throwing color in each ray.

Forming clusters, cheeky bunch,
Always up for a friendly lunch.
In this garden, life stands tall,
Green and happy, a laugh for all.

Succulent Whispers at Dawn

In the twilight, they conspire,
With sleepy heads, they often tire.
Beneath the glow of morning rays,
They giggle soft in gentle plays.

Roots entwined like friends so near,
Sharing jokes only plants can hear.
With every stretch, they greet the day,
Bold and cheeky in their way.

Leaves like laughter, crisp and bright,
Ready to party with the light.
Collecting warmth, like coins to spend,
Cheerful bandits, never end.

In a garden made for fun,
Every hour, a floral pun.
Stop and smile, you'll feel the cheer,
Join their jest, keep laughter near!

Warmth Cradling Cacti

Under the heat, they grin so wide,
Winking at the sun, their pride.
With spines like pickles, oh so bold,
Their stories of warmth are often told.

In a cluster, they plan their schemes,
Basking in light, living the dreams.
Poking fun at what they see,
The cactus crew, so wild and free.

Every inch a prickly jest,
Soft browsers find it quite a test.
Yet within their jokes, there's truth,
Laughing loud, they capture youth.

With sunny days as their best friends,
In greenish laughter, the fun never ends.
Join the feisty, floral bunch,
In this warm embrace, take a punch!

Gift of Light in Clay Pots

In pots so small, they sit and grin,
With leaves like smiles, let the fun begin!
They soak up rays, with joy in tow,
A dance of green in a sunny glow.

Water me, they hold a joke,
A splash on roots, they giggle and poke!
With every sprout, they tease the sun,
In their little world, they always run.

The Music of Green Growth

Tiny fiddles in the breeze,
They strum their strings with charming ease!
Each new leaf sings notes of cheer,
As if the garden's in high gear.

A wind-blown chorus fills the air,
With every sway, they dance with flair!
In pots they rock, in sun they play,
They make the dullest moments sway.

Quiet Spaces in Warmth

In corners bright, they sit and nap,
In silence, they plot their leafy map!
While humans rush, they take their time,
Basking in chill, a perfect rhyme.

They whisper tales of sunlit dreams,
With every sunbeam, their joy redeems.
A comfy couch of soil and light,
They giggle softly, what a delight!

Playful Shadows of Nature

In afternoon, the shadows dance,
On pots and leaves, they waltz and prance!
Each flicker casts a funny show,
A game of tag, where light must go.

They peek and hide behind the stems,
In playful jests, they are all friends.
The sun dips low, the fun won't cease,
In nature's laugh, we find our peace.

Petals of the Day

In pots they dance, these little greens,
With faces turned to light, like sunbeam queens.
They giggle softly, roots in their chair,
Sipping on water, without a single care.

A cactus tried to join the fun,
But he pricked the laughter, oh what a run!
His spines kept dancing, but no one would cheer,
So he sat alone, shedding a tear.

A cheeky jade plant whispered real sly,
"Watch me grow tall, while you just stand dry!"
The others chuckled, in their leafy bliss,
While taking turns at a sun-soaked kiss.

And then the soil dared to giggle aloud,
"I've got the roots, but you're the show, wow!"
So they all basked in the sunny parade,
Awaiting the sunset, unafraid of the fade.

Oasis of Warmth

In a pot of dreams, they gather wide,
Chasing the warmth, with chubby pride.
Poking out arms, they reach for the rays,
Plotting their tricks on sunny days.

One little leaf tried to wear a hat,
But soon it slipped, oh, imagine that!
"I've got style!" it declared in surprise,
As the others laughed, with gleeful eyes.

The little blooms had a dance-off spree,
Waving their petals, oh so carefree!
Twisting and spinning, they jived on the ledge,
While the neighbors peeked, from behind the hedge.

And as shadows crept, and the light did fade,
They chuckled together, in leafy parade.
For in the warm glow, they'd always stay,
Finding the fun in each sunny day.

Nature's Lanterns

Tiny torches glow, a cheerful sight,
Laughing at clouds, chasing away night.
With bellies round, they stretch up high,
Waving hello to the passing sky.

A burro's tail drags, its end quite spry,
As it tickles the toes of those floating by.
"Touchdown!" it squeaks, in a sprightly tone,
While the leaves all giggle, feeling right at home.

Their colors burst forth, a brilliant show,
Making the gray clouds feel rather low.
With joy in their roots, they grin and sway,
Lighting up the garden, come what may.

So there in the beauty of nature's embrace,
These silly plants find their favorite place.
With warmth in their hearts and laughter at will,
They shine like lanterns, on the windowsill.

Basking in Growth

Up on the sill, in a huddle of green,
Life is a laugh, in our little scene.
With big bright smiles, we soak in the glow,
Planting our roots, and letting things flow.

A wedding of leaves in the afternoon,
Swaying to the whispers of a warm tune.
One tried tango, another did jig,
But it fell on the floor, feeling real big!

With a wink from a leaf, and a shrug from a stem,
They celebrated blooms, and shouted, "Ohem!"
Unbothered by shyness, they twirled in delight,
A garden party, till the fall of night.

In pots overflowing, with life and with glee,
Together they bask, as one family.
A chorus of green, full of joy and mirth,
Living and laughing, our comical earth.

Sun-Kissed Serenity

Tiny green friends bask on the sill,
Chasing away worries, they laugh at the chill.
With a wink and a nod, they sway in the light,
These plucky little plants, oh what a sight!

Potted in pairs, they dance in the sun,
With spiky little hairstyles, oh isn't it fun?
Their thirsty thirst whispers, 'Just one more sip!'
While they brace for the noon-day sun's little trip!

Giggling at raindrops, they wiggle with glee,
Each leaf a reminder, be happy and free.
No frowns allowed here, just joy in the day,
In their sunny abode, come jump, come play!

So let's toast to these pals, who thrive with a grin,
In this sunbeam-filled life, let the fun begin!

Thorns and Glow

In the kingdom of green, there's a brave little crew,
With jackets of armor and a vibrant hue.
They poke and they prick, but who could complain?
With faces so silly, dancing in rain!

One says, 'I'm tough, I laugh at the heat!'
While another's just lounging, saying, 'Life's a treat!'
Their party hats sparkle as they jive and they swing,
These little green warriors love to do their thing!

With roots deep in mischief and leaves full of cheer,
They whisper sweet secrets for all plants to hear.
As cacti do shimmy and aloe does twirl,
It's a bright, prickly party in their leafy world!

So join in their laughter, don't take it too slow,
In this patch of delight, it's all thorns and glow!

Drought's Embrace

When the skies are a-dry, and the sun's on a roll,
These little stout heroes laugh, 'We're fun on a stroll!'
With a bounce that's quite cheery and a grin that won't quit,
They face any drought; each leaf is a hit!

"Water, what's that?" they giggle with glee,
"Bring on the hot days, we're wild and so free!"
With roots like a treasure hoard, safe in the sand,
They dance with the breeze, oh, isn't it grand?

In a world that forgets how to smile in the heat,
These nuggets of joy never know defeat.
With each sunny hour, their laughter does swell,
'They call it a drought? Oh, we're just doing well!'

So tiptoe through laughter, where the sunshine creeps,
In this drought of delight, our merriment leaps!

Woven in Warmth

In a basket of colors, with hugs full of laughs,
These quirky little wonders relish their paths.
They twist and they turn, in a sun-dappled spree,
In gardens of whimsy, come dance and be free!

"Oh look at me chubby!" one shouts with a cheer,
"I'm a champion of squishiness, love me, don't fear!"
While others shout, "We're the crown of the sun,
In a world full of green, we know how to have fun!"

With petals that poke and laughter that pricks,
They share all their jokes, with some pokey little tricks.
In the tapestry of joy, they find their own place,
Woven together, each in a funny embrace!

So join the grand party, under skies so bright,
Among these bright buddies, let's dance through the night!

Blades of Green under Sun's Watch

In pots they sit, a joyful crew,
With gentle smiles, they soak up dew.
They wiggle and giggle in the warm air,
No need for sunscreen, they just don't care!

With tiny spines that dance in glee,
They poke each other, such mischief, you see.
A prickly game of hide and seek,
Who knew plants could be so cheeky and sleek?

Each leaf a joke, a pun on the vine,
They make me chuckle, two cups of brine.
A little water, a sprinkle of cheer,
These quirky green pals always draw near.

So here's to the greens, that shimmer and sway,
With their antics, they brighten my day!
Life is a riot, just look at their grin,
In nature's party, where laughter begins.

Daylight's Embrace on Succulent Skin

When morning breaks, they stretch and shine,
Like little stars in a leafy line.
A sunlit tango, a twist and a bounce,
Oh, to join in, I'd dare not flounce!

With laughter that quivers on sun-kissed tips,
Cactus clowns pulling silly flips.
Meanwhile, the ferns shake their leafy tails,
As if spinning tales of wild, green trails.

They huddle close, gossiping in green,
Of wild adventures and places they've been.
A gossip fest that never feels dull,
In this garden of quirk, life's always full!

So let's embrace that sun so bright,
With chuckles and cheers, we'll dance in delight!
For in warm rays, we all can find,
The joy of the day, oh so unconfined.

The Whispering Joy of Green

Whispers of joy through the garden breeze,
Tickled by sunlight, they shimmy with ease.
A cactus jokes about the prickly plight,
While the leaves laugh softly in pure delight.

In a pot party, they share all their dreams,
Sipping on raindrops, or so it seems.
A succulent serenade, sweet and quirky,
They dance in the rays, feeling quite perky.

The aloe dressed up in a glittery gown,
Winks at the aloe, says, "Don't look so down!"
In vibrant hues, they prance and play,
Who knew green could brighten the day?

So bring on the laughter, let it be clear,
These leafy friends spread all the cheer!
In pots full of giggles, what a sight to see,
Life is a garden, let's all just be free!

Golden Glow in Living Portraits

In pots of joy, they line up with flair,
Winking at sunbeams, a glorious affair.
Plant selfies taken with a twisty grin,
Who knew foliage could look so thin?

With a golden glow, they bask in the light,
A parade of colors, too fun and bright!
A succulent's smile is a sight to behold,
As they chat away with tales to be told.

A playful poke, a tumble, a roll,
In this green theater, they all play a role.
With laughter that blossoms in each nook and cranny,
These plants know humor, oh-so uncanny!

So gather 'round for a comedic show,
With leafy performers, enjoy the flow!
In the gallery of life, let happiness pour,
These charming greens keep us wanting more.

Green Retreats in the Sun

I'm a plant with a whimsical grin,
My leaves soak up rays, where do I begin?
Throw me a glass, make it three,
Water's a party, you best come see!

Sipping light like a fancy drink,
In this bright oasis, I never sink.
Standing tall with a spiky flair,
Remind me again, do I need some hair?

Photosynthesis is my favorite game,
Chasing sunbeams, I'll never be tame.
Dragons may breathe fire, that's their lot,
But I'm thriving in gardens, thanks a lot!

So if you're feeling a little drained,
Join the green squad where joy is unchained.
Brighten your space with laughs and glee,
Just don't forget to water me!

Oasis of Radiance

In a pot on the windowsill, I thrive,
With my little green pals, we feel alive.
We gather around, telling tales so dear,
Who knew cactus had such a sense of cheer?

Every little sunbeam, we fightingly chase,
Stretching our arms, making a silly face.
We wiggle and giggle, a happy bunch,
Wondering if sunlight's a tasty lunch!

Each day is a challenge, so much to explore,
Best not forget when the door swings wide,
Look out for the dog, he's trying to hide,
We might be stiff, but we're never a bore!

So come join our team, bring a smile that shines,
In this radiant mood, no need for designs.
Life's better with friends, and with laughter so loud,
In our bright little world, we're forever proud!

Colorful Companions in Nature's Light

A party of plants in dazzling green,
With vibrant hues like you've never seen.
We twirl and bounce in the warm sunlight,
Bringing joy that's simply out of sight!

Each petal a character, distinct, unique,
Some shy and humble, others bold and cheeky.
We're quite the crew, let us have our fun,
Who needs a leash when you're kissed by the sun?

Oh, how we love when the rain drops fall,
Squeezing ourselves up, we stand proud and tall.
While others may wilt on a gloomy day,
We dance and we shimmer in our own bright way!

So gather around for a plant-tastic show,
We promise our humor will steal the glow.
With laughter and light, life's better combined,
In this colorful garden, you'll always find!

Vibrancy of the Arid

Under the sun, we bask without care,
Our spikes are our armor, we flair and dare.
Talk to us softly, we might spill a joke,
In this dry desert, come join the folk!

We wear our best colors, it's quite the show,
While others wilt down, we just go with the flow.
Cracks in the earth? We laugh in delight,
Living it up in this glorious light!

Every groan from the soil, we take in stride,
Our laughter, like pollen, drifts far and wide.
No need for umbrellas, we thrive in the heat,
Dance with the shadows, oh what a treat!

So if you feel low, in a humid mess,
Just look to the pot where we're dressed to impress.
Join our wild antics, the fun never ends,
In the warmth of the arid, you'll find your friends!

Sunlit Serenity

In the corner a pot, green and round,
It wishes to dance, but it's stuck on the ground.
A leaf tickles a friend, they giggle with glee,
Oh, why can't they scoot to the shade of a tree?

They chat and they poke, with roots intertwined,
Dreaming of adventures, their plans seldom aligned.
A pebble rolls by, they plot and they scheme,
But as your best mate, they love you, it seems!

Green Wonders in a Bright World

Tiny green soldiers stand in a row,
Wearing sun hats and shades, putting on a show.
They sip on the light, a drink oh-so-sweet,
With giggles and wobbles, they move their small feet.

When clouds drift above, they jump with delight,
Making faces at shadows, they're quite a sight!
With laughter like rain, they bloom and they sway,
Oh, what a funny game they play every day!

Cacti and Warmth

Prickly and proud, in a bright little nook,
Dreaming of beaches and some silly book.
With arms wide open, they give cactus hugs,
But watch out for needles, those pointy little bugs!

They chat with the sun about their big dreams,
Trading funny stories, bursting at the seams.
At dusk when it's cool, they giggle some more,
As night makes them sparkle, who could ask for more?

The Dance of Light and Leaves

A leaf took a leap, in a breeze with a swirl,
Declaring to flowers, "Come join for a twirl!"
With laughter galore, they kick up some dust,
In the party of greens, it's fun, it's a must!

The sun shines like glitter on each cheeky face,
As they whirl and they giggle, dressed in their grace.
They spin and they sway, a joyful brigade,
In the garden of giggles, never afraid!

Growth in the Glistening

Tiny plants in pots so bright,
Dance around in morning light.
Not a care, they stretch and grow,
Waving to the sun, hello!

Green and plump, they love to play,
Chasing shadows, all the day.
With a sip of water here,
They crack a joke: 'We're in the clear!'

Leaves are laughing in the breeze,
'We're not weeds, we're trophies, please!'
Sharing secrets, roots entwined,
In their world, joy is defined.

So if you seek a little cheer,
Just whisper soft, and they'll appear.
A garden party, no doubt,
With glee and giggles all about!

Light and Life Intertwined

Blushing greens with cheeky grins,
Who knew spikes could be such wins?
They bask and giggle, soak in rays,
Prim and proper in their ways.

Mocking shadows with a wink,
Pots lined up, they never shrink.
'Light a fire, we'll have a ball!'
Who needs a house when plants can haul?

Basking in the warmth so grand,
Practicing the perfect stand.
'Watch us shimmy, wiggle, shake!'
In the glow, they're wide awake.

With sunbeams and a dose of glee,
They toast to life with jubilee.
Grab a drink, join in the fun,
In this party, we're all one!

Desert Blooms in the Golden Glow

In desert lands, where sand does shine,
Dancing blooms, oh, how divine!
Sipping nectar, sweet and light,
Joking with the stars at night.

Cacti wear their spikes with pride,
'Who needs water? We just glide!'
With a giggle, they stand tall,
Braving drought, they steal the call.

A sunny spot, their throne of gold,
'Watch us flourish, proud and bold!'
In a world of dry and hot,
They hold the laughs, they bring the plot.

In golden glow, they dance around,
'The desert's ours! Look what we found!'
Potted dreams in sunshine's play,
They bloom and shine, hip-hip-hooray!

Radiance in Pottery

In earthen homes, they love to sit,
Groovy pots, they've got the wit.
Chillin' out, soaking in blooms,
Catching rays, escaping glooms.

With laughter bright, they make a pact,
'Let's grow wild and never act!'
Pooling together, plants unite,
In this haven, pure delight.

Ceramic smiles and vibrant shades,
'Look at us, we're true cascades!'
Friends forever with roots entwined,
In every hue, joy defined.

So raise your glass to the quick and spry,
With playful hearts, let spirits fly.
In this garden, laughter stays,
As colors dance in sunny rays!

Barefoot Among the Blooms

In fields where little plants wiggle,
I trip and laugh, I take a giggle.
With roots that dance beneath my toes,
They tickle me, oh, how it goes!

The bees buzz by, a tiny choir,
While I play hopscotch on the lyre.
They say I'm nuts for loving leaves,
But who needs shoes? Just watch me weave!

The colors pop, a wild parade,
I skip around this leafy jade.
When petals fall like confetti in June,
I'll catch them all, they're my cartoon!

So here I'll stay, forever free,
With little blooms that laugh with me.
Who needs a hat? Let's paint the town,
With feet exposed, I won't back down!

Reflective Gardens of Joy

Where laughter grows like wild mint sprigs,
I ponder life with silly jigs.
Each leaf a mirror, bright and bold,
Reflecting tales of joy untold.

A cactus stands, a prickly grin,
I chat with it like we're old kin.
It says, 'Don't worry, keep it light!'
So here I stay, day turns to night.

Marigolds giggle, and daisies sway,
As I dance around, come what may.
I ask the clouds to join the show,
Just skip the rain, and let it glow!

In every pot, a secret waits,
The laughter blooms, it celebrates.
With roots sunk deep in happy soil,
I'll dig my joy, I'll never spoil!

Embracing the Day's Warmth

The sun peeks in, a cheeky brat,
Warming up my favorite mat.
I roll around in golden rays,
Like a burrito, happy days!

The silly shadows dance with me,
We twirl around, oh, can't you see?
Each branch above is clapping slow,
These playful leaves all steal the show.

With every giggle, colors flash,
Tiny critters join the bash.
Together we'll create a scene,
Of joy that sparkles, bright and green!

So lift your hands, let's all embrace,
This wacky warm and sunny place.
With every chuckle, every cheer,
Let's soak up all this laughter here!

Festive Greenery Under Sunlit Skies

Under skies that twinkle bright,
I swear the flowers feel all right.
They put on hats, they wave and grin,
As if they know where joy begins.

We organize a garden fest,
Where every leaf is aptly dressed.
The radishes all do the twist,
While petunias chat and coexist!

Each plant has stories, wild and wacky,
With sun-dried smiles, never tacky.
The rubber duck in bloom's parade,
Floats by on laughter, unafraid!

So raise a glass of sunshine cheer,
To all the plants, let's shout and cheer!
With every leaf and pop of bloom,
We paint the world, refusing gloom!

Earth's Embrace of Golden Hues

In pots of green, they dance around,
With laughter loud, they're joy unbound.
Tiny leaves like thumbs that say,
'Look at us, we'll lead the way!'

They sip on rays, a sunny treat,
No need for shoes, they skip the heat.
While humans sweat and fans all whir,
These leafy pals just giggle, purr!

With roots that twirl, they stretch and play,
A jungle gym in grand display.
They sprout with glee, they bloom with cheer,
And whisper jokes for all to hear.

So raise a glass, a toast to green,
To quirky plants, the rare and seen.
In earthly hugs, they sway and sway,
A funny sight, come join, let's play!

The Resilience of Green Hearts

With laughter bright, they greet the day,
Their spiky jokes, oh what a play!
A little drink, they're feeling spry,
They chuckle as the clouds float by.

In drizzles, mumbles, 'Don't you fret,'
With every drop, they laugh and get.
For nature's pranks, they've got no fear,
'We thrive on chaos, keep it near!'

They tease the sunlight, tugging rays,
'You think you're hot? We love these days!'
Their sassy growth, a joyful sight,
While shadows sulk, they steal the light.

With every bloom, they take a chance,
In quirky poses, they all dance.
A garden stage, with humor rife,
The heart of green, a jolly life!

Sunlit Shelters of Life

In cozy corners, they make their stand,
With prickly smiles, oh isn't it grand?
Each leaf a wink, each stem a tease,
They bask and play with joy and ease.

Dancing shadows, they spin around,
While humans trip on solid ground.
In rock and sand, they claim their zone,
A playground rich, they call it home.

With friends of bugs and ants as crew,
They share their thoughts on what to do.
A sip of dew, a wink for show,
'Let's make a garden, go with the flow!'

And if a storm comes knocking fast,
They laugh aloud, 'we'll outlast!'
In sunny smiles, they'll always thrive,
In sunlit shelters, they come alive!

Bright Wonders of the Wild

In wilds so bright, they proudly stand,
With colors bold, like a painter's hand.
They giggle at the curious bees,
'Come taste our nectar, please, if you please!'

With sandy toes and sunny hats,
They throw a bash, invite the brats.
'We're tough and cheery, can't you see?',
They laugh with glee, wild and free.

Watch them grow, a quirky crowd,
With whispers soft, they're always loud.
A roll in dirt, a splash of light,
Bright wonders, what a funny sight!

So join the fun, take a chance,
In lands where green and wild plants dance.
With roots so strong, and hearts like cheer,
These vibrant friends bring laughter near!

Luminescent Gardens at Dusk

Green thumbs wiggle, plants in hand,
They sprout like jokes, in a vibrant band.
Forget-me-nots dance, on a silly breeze,
Tickling petals that bring you to your knees.

The best part of gardening? It's the chat,
With spiky green friends that sit like a cat.
They whisper secrets, in their own way,
Who can resist this leafy ballet?

A cactus named Clyde, with a serious glare,
Claims he's the king, with attitude to spare.
But when the sun sets, he turns into goo,
Rolling in laughter, with the daisies too.

So laugh through the evening, as day turns to night,
These giggling greens make everything right.
In gardens aglow, joy takes its flight,
Under moonlit antics, oh what a sight!

Bright Sentinels of the Sun

Standing tall, in glorious hues,
They wave to the sky, with no time to snooze.
Warring with wind, bending in grace,
Chasing the rays, never leaving their place.

Chubby green pals, no need for a drink,
Telling the raindrops, 'You stink, you stink!'
With cheeky smiles, they soak up the rays,
A jolly parade, in a sunny daze.

When clouds come roaming, they wear little frowns,
But dance like mad when the sun comes round.
A harmony of giggles, in their leafy domain,
Who knew plants could be a punchline campaign?

So here's to the guardians, in their faithful stance,
Making us chuckle, in a leafy dance.
'Neath the sky's laughter, nothing feels dull,
With friends all around, life's beautiful!

Nature's Glorious Workshop

In a workshop of green, with giggles abound,
Nature crafts wonders, all around.
Gluey mud pies and twigs that stick,
Their creations inspire, and add a few tricks.

The tiny plants gather, wielding their tools,
Sketching arrangements, breaking the rules.
They giggle and squeak, snort and play,
Creating their magic, in a funny ballet.

A gopher named Gary, joins in the fun,
Tinkering with pots, oh what's to be done?
With wobbly designs, their laughter grows,
While sculpting the peek-a-boo garden shows.

Here in this space, wild dreams run amok,
Where flowers make hats, and cacti play rock.
Nature's own circus celebrates with a cheer,
As silly inventions bring smiles, my dear!

Tiny Homes of Radiant Life

In mini abodes, green mischief does grow,
These quirky little neighbors put on quite a show.
In pots shaped like cats, or boots made of clay,
Each home bursts with laughter, in its own way.

With twinkling intentions, they wave from their rooms,
Whispering secrets through bright little blooms.
Their party of colors, a whimsical sight,
Fluttering dreamers, twirling in delight.

A lizard named Larry walks on tiptoes,
Peeking in windows to see how it goes.
While a snail takes a tour, all slow and sublime,
Making friends in the garden, taking his time.

In these cozy dwellings, where joy can't be bound,
You'll find party vibes, all around.
So join in their laughter, share giggles and cheer,
In tiny homes where good vibes are near!

Glimmering Greens

In pots they sit, a leafy crew,
With smiles that gleam, they wave to you.
Sometimes they lean, act all aloof,
Joking they're off to the vegetable proof!

One's wearing shades, the other a hat,
Cacti debate—a prickly chat.
"Why does the sun kiss you so sweet?"
"Because I wear sunblock, can't take defeat!"

When it rains, they huddle tight,
Under a roof, they giggle at night.
"Let's throw a party, forget the grime!"
"It's a succulent bash! Pass the thyme!"

So here's to the greens, the quirky kind,
In their sunny world, laughter you'll find.
Think plants can't joke? They surely can!
Let's grab a drink, and make a plan!

Ember and Earth

In a garden plot, with no strict rules,
Little plants plot like sneaky fools.
One igloo's planted, a wishful bloom,
As autumn hints, "I'll bring the gloom!"

They sunbathe daily, but then they lament,
"Where is the rub? Where's our rent?"
The gentle breeze becomes a gust,
"Watch the pots shake, just like us!"

To gather dust, their biggest fear,
"Do you think we'll ever be called deer?"
Quips the jade, "I'll be your queen,
While the sun's ablaze and I'm evergreen!"

So let's toast the earth with a giggle loud,
With pots of green, we're totally proud.
Friends so odd yet totally worth,
A witty bond of ember and earth.

Tender Resilience

On windowsills, they plot and schemes,
Whispers of laughter fill their dreams.
Twirling leaves both bold and spry,
They chuckle at clouds passing by.

One wears a hat, another a shoe,
"Who knew mud pies were good for you?"
"Maybe we should start a trend!"
"No, let's just bloom till we can't bend!"

When evening dawns, they throw a ball,
A serenade in the garden hall.
"Who's got the soil? And pass the tea!"
"Just don't spill it. That's on me!"

Through storms and sun, they dance with cheer,
With roots so strong, they persevere.
The punchline is the best we see,
Life's just great in this leafy spree!

Shimmering Haven

In a patch of light, they jive and sway,
In pots of laughter, they play all day.
"Don't forget to water me!" one cries,
"Or I'll grow legs and run for the skies!"

With branches outstretched, they sing a tune,
"Who invited the moon? Tell it to swoon!"
Loopy leaves, they sway to and fro,
"Join our party, put on a show!"

When raindrops tap, they'll dance in line,
"Life's one great joke, all vines entwine!"
They joke of winter's chilly embrace,
"Wrap us in laughter; we'll win this race!"

So here's to the quirky, the fun-loving bunch,
Who revel in sun, and stay for the lunch.
In this shimmering haven, we find delight,
With plants as pals, everything's right!

Pearls of the Afternoon

In pots and hats, they catch some rays,
Green nubbins dance in sunny ways.
They sip on light, so sweet and bright,
And laugh at cacti with all their might.

Wobbling on a ledge so high,
They roll their eyes at clouds gone by.
"We're the stars of the garden scene!"
They chuckle, as they pose for green.

With every drip from droopy leaves,
They plot to steal the world with ease.
"Watch us twirl and sway with flair,"
They giggle, twinkling in the air.

The afternoon turns pink and gold,
These chubby charms, all bold and cold.
They bask in joy, no care in sight,
As shadows hop to join the light.

Verdant Whispers

In the garden where they grow,
Whispers travel, soft and low.
"Hey there, buddy! Catch some rays?"
Each succulent winks in warm displays.

With plump little arms stretched out wide,
They invite all bugs for a ride.
"Join our party, there's room for more!"
But ants just stare and scurry for the door.

A playful breeze tickles their sides,
While the soil underneath wants to hide.
"We're the jellybeans of the earth!"
They claim with giggles and bursts of mirth.

In the glow of a lazy noon,
They sway and sing their silly tune.
"Life's a joke, but we're no punchline,"
They cheer, as petals intertwine.

Life Beneath the Glow

Underneath the glowing sky,
Chubby plants begin to pry.
"What's the secret to your lift?"
Their leaves whisper, as shadows drift.

A lizard smirks, perched on a rock,
"Don't mind me, I just like to gawk!"
The greens respond with winks and grins,
Their sunny shenanigans begin.

"Some say we're just for the show,
But look at us, we steal the glow!"
They role-play pirates, thieves of light,
With little shouts of pure delight.

Through the dusk, they settle down,
Royal crowns in brown and brown.
"Tomorrow, we'll do it all again!"
As night bows down to their shiny zen.

Sunlit Succor

In a sunny nook, they gather round,
Chubby friends in silence sound.
"Who needs a drink?" one shouts with cheer,
They lean back, basking without fear.

"I forgot my hat," a whisper chimes,
As they discuss their leafy crimes.
The shadows giggle, playing tag,
While their laughter swells like a flag.

Missed a drip? Don't raise a fuss,
They've got each other, that's enough.
"Let's hold a contest of who's the greenest!"
And thus begins their thirst for the meanest.

Drenched in joy, they soak the light,
No frowns allowed; it's pure delight.
Tomorrow brings more playful cheer,
For each soft leaf laughs without fear.

www.ingramcontent.com/pod-product-compliance
Lightning Source LLC
Chambersburg PA
CBHW051643130526
44590CB00068B/2819